REDUCING STRESS

TIM HINDLE

DK PUBLISHING, INC.

A DK PUBLISHING BOOK

Project Editor Sasha Heseltine
Editors Marian Broderick,
David Tombesi-Walton
US Editor Ray Rogers
Designers Elaine C. Monaghan,
Austin Barlow
Assistant Editor Felicity Crowe
Assistant Designer Laura Watson

DTP Designer Jason Little
Production Controller Alison Jones

Series Editor Jane Simmonds
Series Art Editor Jayne Jones

Managing Editor Stephanie Jackson
Managing Art Editor Nigel Duffield

First American Edition, 1998
4 6 8 10 9 7 5 3

Published in the United States by
DK Publishing, Inc.
95 Madison Avenue
New York, New York 10016

Visit us on the World Wide Web at
http://www.dk.com

Library of Congress Cataloging-in-Publication Data
Reducing Stress. -- 1st American ed.
p. cm. -- (Essential Managers)
Includes index.
ISBN 0-7894-2444-4
1. Stress (Psychology). 2. Stress management
3. Job stress. I. Series.
BF575.S75C656 1998   97-38911
155.9'042--DC21   CIP

Reproduced by Colourscan, Singapore
Printed and bound in Italy by Graphicom srl

CONTENTS

4 INTRODUCTION

UNDERSTANDING STRESS

6 WHAT IS STRESS?

10 DEFINING STRESS AT WORK

12 RECOGNIZING SYMPTOMS

14 MEASURING STRESS

16 HOW STRESSED ARE YOU?

ANALYZING THE CAUSES OF STRESS

20 CHANGING SOCIETIES

22 CHANGING ORGANIZATIONS

24 CHANGING PRACTICES

26 ANALYZING JOBS

28 ASSESSING RELATIONSHIPS

30 ASSESSING THE WORKPLACE

32 COPING WITH DAILY LIFE

DEALING WITH STRESS AT WORK

34 IDENTIFYING ATTITUDES

36 DEVISING A STRATEGY

38 TAKING POSITIVE ACTION

40 RECLAIMING YOUR DESK

42 STUDYING WORK PATTERNS

46 MANAGING TIME

48 COMMUNICATING WELL

50 GAINING INNER BALANCE

52 MAKING TIME TO RELAX

54 SEEING STRESS IN OTHERS

56 ANALYZING PERSONALITY

58 HELPING OTHERS

TAKING ACTION AT HOME

62 TAKING TIME OFF

64 LEARNING TO RELAX

66 DEVELOPING INTERESTS

68 IMPROVING DIET

70 INDEX

72 ACKNOWLEDGMENTS

INTRODUCTION

Stress will probably affect all of us at some time in our lives. Reducing Stress will help you manage the stress in your life so that it continues to stretch you toward your personal goals without damaging your health. This book concentrates on minimizing the stress factor in your workplace, with 101 concise tips scattered through the book to give further vital information. Beginning with an analysis of the causes of stress, the book deals with reducing stress in your own life and ends by showing you how to use your newfound knowledge to help others deal with their stress. A self-assessment exercise allows you to plot your stress levels. This book provides invaluable information that you will be able to utilize over and over again as you learn to minimize stress.

UNDERSTANDING STRESS

Stress has been called "the invisible disease." It is a disease that may affect you, your organization, and any of the people in it, so you cannot afford to ignore it.

WHAT IS STRESS?

On occasion, all of us experience stress. Beneficial stress can help drive a few of us to become Olympic champions, but harmful stress can drive others to despair. A force as powerful as that should always be handled with respect.

> **1** Learn how to spot your stress warning signals, and then act on them.

ANALYZING THE EFFECTS OF STRESS

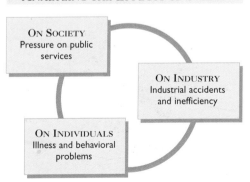

ON SOCIETY
Pressure on public services

ON INDUSTRY
Industrial accidents and inefficiency

ON INDIVIDUALS
Illness and behavioral problems

THE DEFINITION OF STRESS

Stress in individuals is defined as any interference that disturbs a person's healthy mental and physical well-being. It occurs when the body is required to perform beyond its normal range of capabilities. The results of stress are harmful to individuals, families, society, and organizations, which can suffer from "organizational stress."

ITS EFFECT ON SOCIETY

The societal costs of stress are already high – and are increasing steadily. Society bears the cost of public services such as healthcare for those made ill by stress, pensions for early retirement brought on by stress, and disability benefits for accidents occurring because of stress. In addition to this, stress often makes people irritable, and this affects the overall quality of everyone's lives.

2 Do not be afraid to talk about situations that you find stressful.

ITS EFFECT ON COMPANIES

Stress costs industry over $150 billion a year in the US alone through absenteeism and reduced levels of performance by those who are physically present but mentally absent. In the UK, as much as 60 percent of all absenteeism is believed to be caused by stress-related disorders. Anything that can reduce the damaging effects of stress makes workers happier and companies richer.

3 Take a walk when you are stressed – it can help restore your perspective.

ITS EFFECT ON THE BODY

When the human body is placed under physical or psychological stress, it increases the production of certain hormones such as adrenaline and cortisol. These hormones produce marked changes in heart rate, blood-pressure levels, metabolism, and physical activity. Although this physical reaction will help you function more effectively when you are under pressure for short periods of time, it can be extremely damaging to the body in the long run.

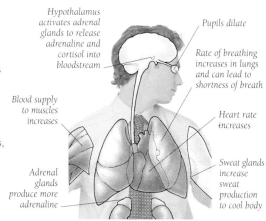

Hypothalamus activates adrenal glands to release adrenaline and cortisol into bloodstream

Blood supply to muscles increases

Adrenal glands produce more adrenaline

Pupils dilate

Rate of breathing increases in lungs and can lead to shortness of breath

Heart rate increases

Sweat glands increase sweat production to cool body

▲ **SYMPTOMS OF STRESS**
The physical symptoms of stress can affect the whole body, particularly the cardiac and respiratory systems.

4 Avoid the habit of taking work home with you every night.

STRESS AND MENTAL HEALTH

The incidence of psychological disorders, such as panic attacks and obsessive behavior, increases with the buildup of long-term stress. Worries can reach such a level that they surface as a frightening, painful physical sensation, which can be mistaken for a heart attack. People under prolonged stress are more prone to irrational fears, mood swings, and phobias and may experience fits of depression, anger, and irritability.

ITS EFFECT ON PHYSICAL HEALTH AND WELL-BEING

Long-term stress has been identified as one of the most prevalent causes of numerous common conditions, including high blood pressure and heart disease. It is now commonly thought that prolonged stress can also increase the risk of psychological or psychiatric ailments. Behavioral changes caused by stress, such as the increased and excessive use of alcohol or drugs, are also linked to a marked decline in physical health.

When under an abnormal amount of stress, the risk of dependency on alcohol is very high. Apart from major physical health problems caused by excessive drinking, overconsumption of alcohol can also result in highly strained and therefore stressful personal relationships, both in the home and at work. Alcohol abuse resulting in worker absenteeism is reckoned to cost the US economy more than $100 billion annually.

Prescribed drugs such as tranquilizers, while sometimes useful in the short term to tackle the symptoms of anxiety, can be addictive and have side effects such as loss of concentration, poor coordination, and dizziness. Tranquilizers, by their very nature, are not a cure for stress since they do not deal with its fundamental causes.

ITS EFFECT ON EMOTIONS

Those who suffer from stress are far more likely to indulge in destructive behavior, which can have a high cost to themselves, to employers, and to society. Typical symptoms such as mood swings and erratic behavior may alienate colleagues as well as friends and family. In some cases, this can start a vicious circle of decreasing confidence, leading to more serious emotional problems, such as depression.

 5 Try to be aware of any changes in your eating and drinking patterns.

ITS EFFECT ON DECISIONS

Suffering from any level of stress can rapidly cause individuals to lose their ability to make sound decisions, especially if their self-confidence fails. This affects health, family, and career alike, since stress in one area of life inevitably affects others. Someone suffering from stress may not heed physical signs of illness, attributing them to the side effects of stress. Faulty decisions made in the workplace and at home may lead to accidents or arguments, financial loss, or even the loss of a job.

> **6** "Talk truth to power" – do not be afraid to tell your supervisor what really goes on in the office.

POINTS TO REMEMBER

- Stress can be a killer. The Japanese have an officially recognized condition called *karoshi* – death from stress caused by too much work.
- Suffering from stress should not be considered a sign of weakness.
- Stress is infectious. It is stressful to live and work with people who are suffering from stress.
- Stress is produced by high demands in life combined with high constraints and little support from colleagues or family.
- There is no formula guaranteeing a stress-free life, but there are techniques for minimizing stress.

ITS EFFECT ON FAMILIES

Stress can break up homes and families. The high divorce rates in the West are due partly to the rapid increase in stress in the workplace, especially where both partners are working full time. It is difficult to find the energy to be supportive to family and friends if work is very difficult or you are afraid that you may lose your job.

When children are involved, stress can cause a conflict relating to child care and careers. Although we do not yet fully understand the long-term impact of separation or divorce on children, we know that it is not the best way to create a generation of stress-free individuals. This requires a very careful balance of the demands of work and home.

◀ SORTING OUT PRIORITIES
Stress is caused by a failure to balance conflicting demands. Juggling work commitments, social life, and child care may mean that not enough time or energy can be devoted to any one activity.

DEFINING STRESS AT WORK

Changes in working practices, such as the introduction of new technology or the alteration of targets, may cause stress, or stress may be built into an organization's structure. Organizational stress can be measured by absenteeism and quality of work.

7 Next time you feel you have too much to do, delegate at least one task.

8 Learn from those who do not suffer from stress.

9 Avoid routinely working late and on weekends.

ORGANIZATIONAL STRESS

Stress affects organizations as well as the individuals within them. An organization with a high level of absenteeism, rapid staff turnover, deteriorating industrial and customer relations, a worsening safety record, or poor quality control is suffering from organizational stress. The causes may range from unclear or overlapping job descriptions to lack of communication to poor working conditions, including "sick building syndrome." This is when a lack of ventilation, insufficient lighting, and inadequate insulation in a building contribute to consistently high levels of illness and absenteeism.

COUNTING THE COST OF WORKPLACE STRESS

Stress causes problems, and these problems cost organizations in different ways:

- Low quality of service. An increase in complaints and lost customers costs time and money. Complaints take time to deal with, and replacement products or services cost money. Loss of customers endangers a company.
- High staff turnover. Both time (for retraining) and money (for recruitment) are spent on replacing unhappy workers.

- Poor reputation. A company with dissatisfied customers will need to pay for changes to restore confidence in its products and services.
- Poor organizational image. A company may recruit only a low-quality – or inexperienced – workforce, since high-fliers are unlikely to be attracted to it.
- Dissatisfied workers. Valuable time is spent in disputes with management over terms and conditions of employment.

SENIOR MANAGER

Anxious about company's annual results

◀ FOLLOWING THE PATH OF STRESS THROUGHOUT AN ORGANIZATION

This chart shows one example of the structure of a department in an organization, indicating typical causes of stress that may affect staff at certain levels in the structure and particular causes that are affecting individuals. Stress is contagious: anyone who is not performing well due to stress increases the amount of pressure on their colleagues, superiors, and subordinates.

Demands of superior and subordinates may conflict.

MANAGER

Involved in detailed arrangements for forthcoming business trip

MANAGER

Anticipating promotion, since senior manager is due to retire

Personality clashes may affect workers at the same level in the hierarchy.

SUBORDINATE

Working hard to finish project before going on vacation

SUBORDINATE

New recruit, not yet familiar with culture of company

Inexperience may cause staff to make errors in judgment.

Lack of involvement in decisions can be a source of resentment.

SUBORDINATE

Concerned that she is not advancing as fast as colleagues

Lacks confidence in meetings

SUBORDINATE

SUBORDINATE

Overeager to progress, so may not listen to superiors

RECOGNIZING SYMPTOMS

There is no single symptom that can identify stress – stressed and unstressed people may equally well have heart disease or drink to excess. A common factor in stressed individuals is the presence of a number of symptoms.

PHYSICAL SIGNS

Some physical symptoms of stress can be life-threatening, such as high blood pressure and heart disease. Less life-threatening physical signs include insomnia, a feeling of constant fatigue, headaches, skin rashes, digestive disorders, ulcers, colitis, loss of appetite, overeating, and cramps. Many of these occur at some point after a stressful event. Other symptoms of stress are more immediate – for example, feelings of nausea, breathlessness, or a dry mouth. All these symptoms, of course, may be caused by factors other than stress. If you or a colleague are naturally prone to headaches, for example, be wary of jumping to inaccurate conclusions about stress levels.

10 If you suffer from regular headaches or insomnia, see a doctor.

11 Make a note of anything that you can find that helps you relax.

Eyes are bloodshot and puffy

Clothing is disheveled

Posture is slouched

◀ RECOGNIZING STRESS AT WORK
It is often quite easy to spot signs of stress in the people you work with. Some of the more common symptoms include a marked decline in personal appearance, a quick and fiery temper, changes in eating habits, and a general withdrawal from social activities.

EMOTIONAL SIGNS

The emotional symptoms of stress can include general irritability, acute anxiety attacks, depression, lack of libido, the loss of a sense of humor, and an inability to concentrate on the simplest of routine tasks. Understanding unusual emotional responses and related changes in behavior is the key to recognizing stress in yourself and others. Some of the most common indications of stress are:

- Becoming unnecessarily overemotional or aggressive in conflict situations;
- Loss of interest in personal appearance, other people, social events, or previously enjoyed activities, such as a favorite sport;
- Poor concentration, difficulty in remembering, and an inability to make decisions;
- Sadness, guilt, fatigue, apathy, and a pronounced feeling of helplessness or failure;
- Loss of confidence in personal ability, often coupled with a lack of self-worth.

12 Listen to what your body tells you as objectively as you can.

POINTS TO REMEMBER

- Family, friends, and colleagues often spot signs of stress before the affected individual does.
- Hobbies and interests are healthy mood enhancers; their absence, especially if sudden, may worsen underlying stress.
- Almost everyone has a certain weakness that comes to the fore when they are stressed. For example, many resume smoking even though they "quit" before.

BEHAVIORAL SYMPTOMS

As a temporary relief from stress, many people indulge to excess in eating, smoking, drinking, or spending. Stress can turn an occasional smoker into a chain smoker and the social drinker into an alcoholic. Individuals may not recognize they are overindulging; those who do may go to some lengths to keep their self-destructive behavior from friends, family, and colleagues.

ABUSING STIMULANTS ▷
Sugar, alcohol, nicotine, and caffeine can all help overcome fatigue, anxiety, and tension rapidly – but all too briefly. Used to excess, they heighten the symptoms caused by stress.

Alcohol consumption can creep up imperceptibly

Chocolate provides a short-term sugar high

Smoking may increase with stress levels

Caffeine consumption may rise rapidly

MEASURING STRESS

There are a number of elements that can be quantified and used as approximate measures of stress levels. These elements vary according to whether stress is being measured in an individual, in an organization, or in society itself.

13 Ask yourself if other people find you stressful to work with.

14 Keep a diary of the days that you feel highly stressed.

LOOKING AT STATISTICS

One of the most useful sources of information on the level of stress in society is national statistics – for example, the annual rate of heart attacks and suicides. Changes over a period of time in these statistics are particularly significant, since they highlight trends. An increase in heart attacks or suicides usually reflects a major social cause of stress in a country, such as widespread unemployment or economic catastrophe.

MEASURING STRESS IN INDIVIDUALS

Although stress in individuals can be measured to some extent by things like heart rate and the level of adrenaline production, it has more to do with how far "out of sync" an individual is with their usual physical condition. Since everyone has a different heart rate or blood pressure, there is no average statistic to indicate personal stress. Also, different people respond differently to stress. In some, stress can manifest itself in panic attacks, headaches, or stomach problems. Others may suffer a lack of sleep or a loss of self-esteem. There are also thought to be different responses for men and women. Whereas women may become withdrawn or depressed, men are more likely to become aggressive, irritable, or develop addictions.

STRESS STATISTICS

The following statistics attest to some of the effects of stress:
- Stress-related problems are thought to cause half of all premature deaths in the US.
- In the EC, some 10 million people suffer from work-related illness each year.
- In Norway, work-related sickness costs 10 percent of the Gross National Product.
- In the UK, 180 million work days per year are lost through stress in the workplace.

MEASURING STRESS IN ORGANIZATIONS

Companies and other types of organization have certain widely recognized quantitative measures of the level of stress, the most popular of which is the absenteeism figure. This is the percentage of staff absent from work on any one day. However, you cannot deduce that the company with the highest rate of absenteeism is necessarily the most stressed; certain industries are more prone to absenteeism, through injury for example. In fact, many companies suffer from "presenteeism," the presence of disaffected or exhausted workers of no more benefit to the company than absentees. Increasingly, those suffering from stress choose to go to work rather than stay at home.

15 Treat yourself to something you want but would not normally buy.

16 Make sure your desk is as near a window as possible.

MEASURING STRESS LEVELS

TYPE OF STRESS	ELEMENTS THAT CAN BE MEASURED
SOCIETAL STRESS This is visible in society as a whole, manifesting itself with a decline in general behavior.	● Unexpected changes in crime figures. ● Unemployment figures, with special regard to inner-city areas in which unemployment may be endemic. ● Educational results, especially in schools in poor rural and run-down inner-city areas. ● Levels of emigration and immigration.
PERSONAL STRESS This causes individuals to suffer a lack of both control and ability to function on a reasonable level.	● Persistent insomnia. ● Rashes, cramps, headaches, or other physical symptoms of unknown origin. ● Changes in eating patterns. ● Marked rise in a personal level of cigarette, alcohol, and drug consumption.
ORGANIZATIONAL STRESS This affects the general morale of an organization, resulting in both financial and personnel problems.	● Unexpected changes in levels of absenteeism among employees. ● Quality of production within the organization, with the emphasis on apparent decline. ● Number of work-related accidents. ● Number of work-related health complaints.

HOW STRESSED ARE YOU?

The first hurdle to beating stress is recognizing its existence – acknowledging that stress is a problem is a vital step toward reducing it. Measure your level of stress regularly by responding to the following statements, then mark the options closest to your experience. Be as honest as you can: if your answer is "never," mark Option 1; if it is "always," mark Option 4; and so on. Add your scores together, then refer to the Analysis to see how you scored. Use your answers to identify the areas that need improving.

OPTIONS

1 Never

2 Sometimes

3 Often

4 Always

1 I blame myself when things go wrong at work.

| 1 | 2 | 3 | 4 |

2 I bottle up my problems, then feel like I want to explode.

| 1 | 2 | 3 | 4 |

3 I concentrate on my work to forget about personal problems.

| 1 | 2 | 3 | 4 |

4 I take out anger and frustration on those nearest to me.

| 1 | 2 | 3 | 4 |

5 I notice negative changes in my behavioral patterns when I am under pressure.

| 1 | 2 | 3 | 4 |

6 I focus on the negative rather than the positive aspects of my life.

| 1 | 2 | 3 | 4 |

7 I feel uncomfortable when experiencing new situations.

1 2 3 4

8 I feel that the role I play within my organization is worthless.

1 2 3 4

9 I arrive late for work or important meetings.

1 2 3 4

10 I respond negatively to personal criticism.

1 2 3 4

11 I feel guilty if I sit down and do nothing for an hour or so.

1 2 3 4

12 I feel rushed, even if I am not under pressure.

1 2 3 4

13 I have insufficient time to read newspapers as often as I would like.

1 2 3 4

14 I demand attention or service immediately.

1 2 3 4

15 I avoid expressing my true emotions both at work and at home.

1 2 3 4

16 I undertake more tasks than I can handle at once.

1 2 3 4

17 I resist taking advice from colleagues and superiors.

1 2 3 4

18 I ignore my own professional or physical limitations.

1 2 3 4

19 I neglect my hobbies and interests because my work takes up all my time.

1 2 3 4

20 I tackle situations before thinking them through thoroughly.

1 2 3 4

21 I am too busy to have lunch with friends and colleagues during the week.

1 2 3 4

22 I put off confronting and resolving difficult situations when they arise.

1 2 3 4

23 People take advantage of me when I do not act assertively.

1 2 3 4

24 I am embarrassed to say when I feel overloaded with work.

1 2 3 4

25 I avoid delegating tasks to other people.

1 2 3 4

26 I deal with tasks before prioritizing my workload.

1 2 3 4

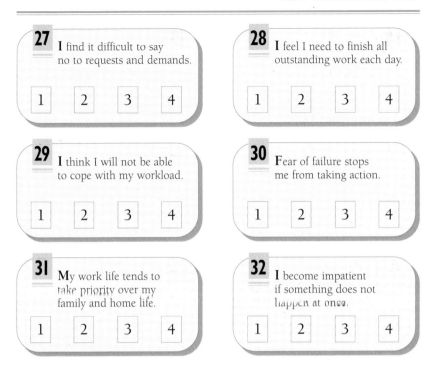

27 I find it difficult to say no to requests and demands.

| 1 | 2 | 3 | 4 |

28 I feel I need to finish all outstanding work each day.

| 1 | 2 | 3 | 4 |

29 I think I will not be able to cope with my workload.

| 1 | 2 | 3 | 4 |

30 Fear of failure stops me from taking action.

| 1 | 2 | 3 | 4 |

31 My work life tends to take priority over my family and home life.

| 1 | 2 | 3 | 4 |

32 I become impatient if something does not happen at once.

| 1 | 2 | 3 | 4 |

ANALYSIS

Now that you have completed the self-assessment, add up your total score and check your stress level by reading the corresponding evaluation. However low your stress level may be, there is always room for improvement. Identify your weakest areas, then refer to the relevant sections in this book. Here you will find practical advice and tips to reduce your own stress levels and minimize any stress-inducing factors in your work environment.

32–64: You manage your stress level very well. Too little stress can be unstimulating, so strive to achieve the optimum balance between positive and negative stress.

65–95: You have a reasonably safe level of stress, but certain areas need improvement.

96–128: Your level of stress is too high. You need to develop new strategies to help reduce it.

ANALYZING THE CAUSES OF STRESS

Society, the working world, and daily life have changed
almost beyond recognition in the past 50 years. These
changes have contributed to a major increase in stress.

CHANGING SOCIETIES

*Demographic change has been dramatic
in recent years. Changes include rapid
population growth, migration from rural
areas to cities, a rise in the number of elderly
people, and the developing role of women. All
these changes have increased stress levels.*

 17 Use travel time
to plan your day
or switch off – not
to do extra work.

INCREASING URBANIZATION

The most stressful change in recent decades has
been rapid urbanization. In some industrialized
countries, such as the Netherlands and Germany,
more than 80 percent of the population lives in
cities. Stress arises from cramped living conditions,
the proximity of millions of other people, and high
levels of crime, noise, and air pollution.

◀ **POPULATION INCREASE**
*It took thousands of years before our planet
boasted one billion people. Now the population
increases by over one billion per decade.*

AGING POPULATIONS

Life expectancy is increasing – people live longer than ever before. This is due to better diet and a rapid improvement in medical knowledge over the past 200 years. The fall in the birth rate (especially in urban areas) means that the world's industrial nations now have an aging population – an increasing proportion of over-60s. On an individual level, this may be stressful when there is conflict between career plans and long-term care for aging relatives. The cost to society is also increasing as healthcare costs continue to spiral.

▼ **CHANGES IN WORLD POPULATION**
The charts below show how the average age of the world's population changed in a 50-year period. From 1950 to 2000, the population pyramid turns upside down, ending up with the largest slice of the population aged between 50 and 64 years instead of under the age of 30.

Key

 10 million men   *10 million women*

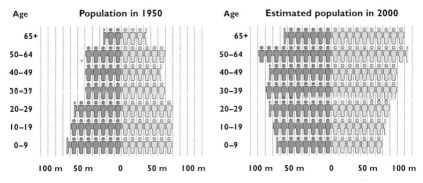

Age	Population in 1950	Age	Estimated population in 2000
65+		65+	
50–64		50–64	
40–49		40–49	
30–39		30–39	
20–29		20–29	
10–19		10–19	
0–9		0–9	

100 m   50 m   0   50 m   100 m   100 m   50 m   0   50 m   100 m

18 Spend an hour or two alone each week, away from work and family.

CHANGING GENDER ROLES

The role of women has changed dramatically over the past 100 years, especially in urban societies. As women make up a greater part of the total labor force, they are judged by the same criteria and put under the same stresses as men. However, women often suffer more stress than their male colleagues because of conflict between work outside the home and work within the home, where they may continue to shoulder the main responsibility for traditional female roles. These changing roles also challenge male identity and work patterns as women take on jobs traditionally held by men.

CHANGING ORGANIZATIONS

In recent years, many companies have launched new products or services while also making cutbacks. Such changes can be vital to a company's survival, but employees may find themselves working harder than ever and facing an uncertain future.

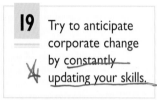

19 Try to anticipate corporate change by constantly updating your skills.

THE LANGUAGE OF CHANGE

ACQUISITION: the purchase by one company of the controlling interest in another.

ALLIANCE: a connection between two organizations for their mutual benefit.

FLATTENING: widening the scope of jobs by compressing organizational hierarchy.

GLOBALIZING: marketing products or services worldwide.

MERGER: the combining of two or more organizations into one.

PRIVATIZING: selling a state-owned firm to the private sector.

QUALITY MANAGING: setting up company systems to monitor product quality.

REENGINEERING: completely rethinking and redesigning organizational processes.

RESTRUCTURING: reorganizing the structure and processes of work within an organization.

RESPONDING TO PRESSURE

The upheaval triggered by the need for cost-cutting and increasing productivity has two main causes:

● Globalization has left local suppliers facing stiff competition and led to aggressive cost-cutting in the marketplace;

● Information technology, including fax machines, e-mail, and video conferencing, has accelerated the speed at which many business transactions can be performed and put pressure on the workforce to be ever more productive.

RETHINKING COMPANIES

New competition and pressures on companies to be more productive have led them to pursue certain strategies that put their workers under stress. Mergers and acquisitions between corporations have been taking place at an increasing rate and, when these occur, they usually bring job losses. This is because they tend to create one large corporation in which key positions at many levels are duplicated, making job cuts inevitable.

20 Adopt new management ideas only if they are useful – never adopt what is merely fashionable.

CHANGING OPERATIONS

In the search for improvement, companies look closely at how they operate – the way production processes work, for example, and ways of keeping track of stock. Many companies have experimented with reengineering their structures and involving employees in controlling product quality and ensuring continuous improvement.

The introduction of robots on to assembly lines has eliminated many manual jobs once required for mass production, so that manufacturing jobs are often relatively isolated with little social contact.

21 Protect your job by drawing attention to the value of your work.

ENCOUNTERING NEW WORK CULTURES

The changes occurring in the workplace in recent years have radically altered the work culture of many companies, large and small. For example, opportunistic takeovers have put old-fashioned organizations into the hands of ambitious and fast-moving entrepreneurs with very different values. Widespread privatization has turned state-owned enterprises into private enterprises, which tend to be more committed to maximizing profit than to maintaining the workforce.

22 Take advantage of training programs to learn as much as you can about new or different work cultures.

REACHING THE LIMITS

All these changes in the workplace – technical, strategic, operational, and cultural – have had profound and far-reaching effects on the employees of the organizations that undergo them. A number of studies have pointed out that, although workers are adaptable, there are limits to the amount of change that human beings can absorb. If organizations keep reaching and exceeding these limits – moving the goalposts – they may find that eventually their workers can no longer tolerate the demands made of them.

23 Identify like-minded colleagues, then work with them to adapt to change.

CHANGING PRACTICES

Change is less stressful when anticipated. Keep abreast of recent developments within your industry, familiarize yourself with new technology, try to gain experience of as many different skills as possible, and maximize the options available to you.

24 Be prepared to change careers at least once in your working life.

REASSESSING MARKETS

The ability to anticipate change depends on recognizing shifts in supply and demand in the labor market. This is not easy, if only because the advent of computers has meant that changes occur much more rapidly than in the past. There are, however, a few key communication and computer technologies, including the Internet and multimedia, that are widely available and drive many other developments. Keeping abreast of changes within these technologies can maximize job prospects and minimize stress by giving you the ability to change with the employment market.

25 When learning new technology, start slowly and build confidence.

UNDERSTANDING NEW TECHNOLOGY

Computers are fundamental to 99 percent of the world's businesses. But many senior managers who are responsible for purchasing hardware and deciding how to use it have scant knowledge of how much it can do. Courses covering all stages are available to help you improve your computer skills – utilize them, since computer literacy is essential for employees at all levels.

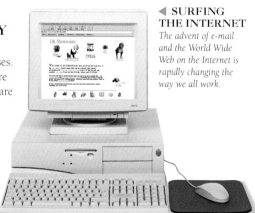

◀ **SURFING THE INTERNET**
The advent of e-mail and the World Wide Web on the Internet is rapidly changing the way we all work.

RELOCATING OFFICES

Information technology provides more flexibility in the way we work today by enabling individuals to decide how and where they work. Those whose jobs require little more than a computer and a phone can work as easily in an airport lounge or the back seat of a car as in a traditional office. Many people now choose to work at home. In this way they can work without the usual interruptions while avoiding the cumulative stress of commuting and reducing travel costs. Everyday chores such as shopping and settling bills are increasingly being carried out by computer from home offices.

26 Try to set up an office near other people: isolation can be stressful.

WORKING FROM HOME ▶
Try to locate your home office in a room set aside for that purpose, as far as possible from living and sleeping areas so you can leave work behind at the end of the day. Many people who work at home convert a spare bedroom into an office.

27 Make sure your home office is separate from your living space.

28 It is never too late to learn a new skill such as computing.

DIVERSIFYING CAREERS

One spin-off from the rapid changes occurring in the workplace is the opportunity to enjoy several different careers during a lifetime. Traditionally, people learned a trade or profession that they then practiced throughout their working life. Today, the demand for skills is changing so fast that this is no longer very likely to happen.

Adaptability and flexibility are vital to minimize the stress of job loss. Anticipate changes, and be prepared for them wherever possible. Retrain if necessary, and look on an unexpected job loss as an "opportunity," allowing you to pursue a new career doing something that really interests you.

ANALYZING JOBS

Some jobs are intrinsically more stressful than others. Jobs at different levels within the hierarchy of an organization each have their own stress factors. Likely stress levels are an important consideration when deciding if a job is suitable for you.

29 Assess the stress factors of any new job before you accept it.

LEVELS OF STRESS IN DIFFERENT JOB TYPES

TYPES OF JOB	RELATED CAUSES OF STRESS
FINANCIAL Accountants, stock-market traders, mortgage consultants, bank tellers.	In companies where money is the major product, a high level of stress is a permanent feature. The larger the amounts involved, the greater the stress on the staff.
SALES-ORIENTED Sales and marketing managers and consultants, advertising executives.	These jobs pressurize workers by continually demanding that they reach targets within certain budgets and deadlines. Salespeople are constantly "on show."
TECHNOLOGICAL Computer programmers and technicians, statisticians.	Information-technology specialists need to keep abreast of the fastest-changing industry ever. Technicians need to fix hardware and explain complex problems to the uninitiated.
MEDIA Newspaper, magazine, or television journalists, producers, editors.	Periods of calm are interspersed with frantic bursts of activity as media workers hunt for new subject material and are then required to be creative under tight deadlines.
MEDICAL Nurses, doctors, anesthetists, pharmacists, physical therapists.	When people's health and even lives are at stake, there can be enormous pressure to make the right decision quickly. There is great stress in dealing with human distress.
PEOPLE-BASED Personnel managers, social workers, counselors, any managers with a team of staff working under them.	These jobs require skills such as tact and discretion that can make it difficult to socialize with colleagues. It may be necessary to implement job reductions, disciplinary procedures, and other decisions that cause people distress.

Stress in Management

Frequently, managers find themselves in isolated positions. They are often caught between trying to satisfy the needs of their staff on the one hand and fulfilling the wishes of their superiors on the other. They also need to make difficult decisions about the future of their staff. Managers require a number of people skills, which may be difficult to define. A feeling that you lack these skills is stressful, as is an inability to delegate, an inability to say "no," a sense of ambiguity about your supposed role, and too much responsibility.

Motivating staff

Meeting deadlines

Staying within budgets

Reporting to superiors

Adapting to change

▲ DEMANDS ON A MANAGER

Too many demands and too much responsibility placed on one person can result in high stress levels. Many managers regard stress as a normal part of working life, but without adequate time for relaxation, stress can lead to illness and even death.

30 Gradually increase the number and complexity of tasks you delegate successfully every day.

Finding little variety in daily tasks

Being uncertain about career prospects

Having no control over workload

Lacking in financial incentives

Feeling the lack of job status

▲ STRESSES ON A CLERICAL WORKER

Many clerical jobs are so repetitive and undemanding that the worker receives very little job satisfaction. There is too little responsibility and therefore a lack of potential for creativity. The boredom and lethargy thus induced can be highly stressful and difficult to shake off.

Stress at Other Levels

Junior white-collar workers may suffer from the stress of too little responsibility and not enough control over a heavy and tedious workload. An employee on a production line may become ill as a result of unstimulating, repetitive work. Stress among manual laborers can often be caused by the physical demands of their jobs, such as dangerous or high-level work on a building site.

ASSESSING RELATIONSHIPS

Poor relationships with colleagues at work can cause stress. Try to analyze relationships that could be improved and identify any problem areas. Is it difficult to control your subordinates, for example, or are superiors distant and unappreciative?

31 Treat all staff with dignity and respect, regardless of their positions or titles.

32 Give coworkers a treat to show your appreciation.

33 Have lunch with a new colleague to establish a working relationship.

EXPERIENCING CHANGE

New organizational structures lay great emphasis on teamwork. The rapid growth of information technology can make middle managers obsolete by reducing their function as communicators of information through an organization. Letting go of such managers and the consequent change in corporate hierarchy are part of a process known as "flattening." Stress in a flattened company can arise because more people find themselves working at a similar level of seniority, and this can lead to greater competition. Employees are working more closely with their colleagues than before, and their roles in a team can often overlap. The success of a smooth-running and happy team depends on cooperation. If this is not present, conflict is likely.

CULTURAL DIFFERENCES

The opportunities for misunderstanding that arise when working with people from other countries can be intensely stressful.

If you do business with a society that is culturally different from yours, familiarize yourself with the values espoused by that society. For example, in Europe and the US, the age of senior staff is regarded as largely irrelevant – in fact, youth is seen as being linked to energy. In East Asia, however, age is respected because it is linked with experience and wisdom. Senior managers may not expect to have dealings on an equal basis with a younger person, and you should always be sensitive to this when negotiating with someone of a different age.

OBSERVING RELATIONSHIPS

Despite corporate restructuring, relationships at work are still largely influenced by hierarchy and by the level of cohesiveness in a group. Factors such as length of service and different skill areas play a crucial role in such work relationships. Look around your office: who goes to whom for help? Who socializes together? Is anybody isolated, and do you know why? Are there any rivalries?

34 Introduce yourself to other people in your company by visiting their offices.

DEALING WITH FELLOW WORKERS

MANAGER
As a manager it is inevitable that you will come into contact with people on all levels. Keep lines of communication open at all times to avoid stressful misunderstandings and any resulting conflict.

SUPERIOR
Is your superior a reader (prefers written reports) or a listener (prefers verbal information)? Communicate in the way they prefer to maintain good relations.

COLLEAGUE
Team members may be competing with you for promotion. If you work together, be aware of any conflict of interest, and do not assume you share the same priorities.

SUBORDINATE
Gain respect from subordinates by treating them as equals. Encourage two-way dialogue so that they know what is going on and can make a positive contribution.

ANALYZING PROBLEMS

Layers of formality at work may make it difficult to confront a relationship problem, but failure to do so means bottling it up, which can be very stressful.

First, you need to identify the basic cause of the problem, then talk to someone who understands the situation and can help. Common problems between people include no feedback on decisions, office politics, uncertainty about roles, unreasonable deadlines, and personality clashes. Once you have analyzed the problem, you can decide on a solution.

35 Share the trip to work with a colleague who lives nearby.

Assessing the Workplace

The structure of an organization and its day-to-day workplace conditions can have a major effect on stress levels. Take a long, hard look at both areas to help identify what is putting you or your colleagues under stress, then work out the best solutions.

36 Always be flexible in your attitudes – you may not know the full story.

Knowing Your Company

Do you agree with the way your company does business? Do you feel comfortable with its policies, structure, and hierarchy? If the answer to any of these questions is "no," you are in a stress-creating situation. It may seem that the easiest thing to do is just to leave an organization if you dislike its structure, but such a radical move is in itself very stressful. It is better to familiarize yourself with all the information you can about the areas you do not like and to learn the reasons behind the way the company is organized and run. Having armed yourself with all the facts, you can then become involved in suggesting improvements from within.

37 Play an active part in improving the quality of office life.

38 Do not make major decisions too quickly.

TREADING ▶ GENTLY

Sharon's attempts to change company policy were vetoed by her boss, putting her in a stressful situation. After learning more about the company, she realized that her original ideas were too radical. She went on to develop successful new products by building on the company's existing strengths.

CASE STUDY

Sharon was appointed the new product development manager at Tiny Tim Toys, makers of quality toys for children. She was faced with a rigid marketing policy and declining sales. The directors constantly rejected her new product ideas, and after several months she became very frustrated.

Under pressure to come up with ideas that the board would find acceptable, she discussed the company's past successes with the sales director, then spoke to the sales representatives to see how the company's products were viewed by toy stores. She then produced a report showing that Tiny Tim Toys was respected by retailers but was seen as unexciting.

The board gave Sharon the go-ahead to update its most successful line of toys, and sales figures slowly began to improve.

IMPROVING CONDITIONS

A poor working environment can be a major cause of stress. Not only does it affect the way you do your job, but it can also undermine your health. Assess working conditions using the checklist below. If conditions need improving, make the changes that you can implement, then ask your organization to make it a priority to make further improvements if necessary:

- Are the desks arranged to maximize space?
- Is there noise or other pollution?
- Is there enough natural light?
- Is there enough storage and filing space? Do colleagues put things back where they belong?
- Is the temperature consistently comfortable? Is it controlled artificially? Does the air conditioning work well? Does it make noise?
- Is the office equipment sophisticated enough to deal with the tasks being set?
- Is there a support network in place in case computer, electrical, or other systems fail?

POINTS TO REMEMBER

- Maintaining a pleasant working environment shows the company cares for its employees, giving a better image to visitors.
- Good use of space allows each person some privacy, even within open-plan offices.
- Natural light can lift moods and prevent eye strain.
- Investing in good storage systems cuts down on the time wasted looking for lost papers or files.
- Potted plants improve humidity in dry air-conditioned offices.
- Adjustable chairs help prevent back pain, a major cause of absenteeism among office staff.
- Repairing or replacing faulty office equipment improves efficiency and productivity.

MAKING ▶ CHANGES
If necessary, rearrange the layout of an office to create a more relaxed environment. Try to strike a balance between allowing easy contact and providing privacy. Set aside a table for meetings in a quiet area so that distractions are kept to a minimum.

COPING WITH DAILY LIFE

Many people believe that they have no choice but to work all the hours available. This belief may be reinforced if work is used to escape from other problems. Be aware of your needs, and try to develop a fulfilling private life as well as a career.

39 Attempt to have lunch with your partner or a close friend once a week.

DEALING WITH CHANGE

Life events can suddenly disrupt a happy balance between work and home. A change of job is an obvious example; events such as marriage or the death of a parent may also undermine this balance.

When stressful changes occur, take time to reassess your lifestyle. Draw up a list of your priorities. You may know what is important in your life, but you may have difficulty in accepting or seeing the implications. "My children are the most important thing in the world to me," says many a manager who sees them on just one night a week. Use change as a positive way to reorder your life.

▲ FORMING CLOSE BONDS
Building a happy family life and establishing a close circle of friends can prove to be a successful way to avoid stress.

MEASURING STRESS ▶
Research has revealed that the death of a partner is at the top of the list of life's most stressful events. Even positive events such as marriage can cause tremendous stress. Experiencing a number of major life events in a short period of time greatly increases the risk of stress.

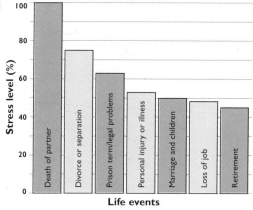

COPING WITH LIFE EVENTS

Aside from death and divorce, there are a number of other life experiences that can cause high stress levels. These include moving, having a baby (for both mother and father), taking a job in a foreign country, and retiring from work. Such events all involve major change, a break in daily routine, and often a series of goodbyes.

To minimize the stress caused by such an event, do not pretend that it has not happened, but try to reduce the uncertainty involved. Visit the foreign job site before you move. Take retirement gradually by working two days a week initially. Take at least a week off work to move. Use up any paid or unpaid leave. Take time and care to say goodbye.

40 Listen carefully to what your children say to you.

41 If you live near your work, walk or cycle to work a few times a week.

COMMUTING TO WORK

Our daily journeys to and from work are among the most stressful regular events in our lives. Worries about punctuality, traffic jams, and overcrowded trains and buses are experienced on a repeated basis, and over weeks and months this can lead to an accumulation of stress.

Think carefully about whether you can rearrange your travel so that it occurs outside the usual rush hours. If possible, work at home for an hour or two in the morning. Arranging flexible working hours allows you to avoid peak travel times by arriving at work late or early, reducing the stress linked to time pressure and punctuality.

▲ COMMUTING BY CAR

If it is important that you arrive somewhere at a specific time, do not travel by road. Today's traffic jams make the car the least reliable form of transportation – as well as the most antisocial. Use an alternative method of transportation where possible.

42 Learn to talk openly about your emotions and feelings with close friends and confidants.

DEALING WITH STRESS AT WORK

Everybody responds to stress in a different way. It is only by understanding the nature of individual responses that you can start fighting stress in yourself and others.

IDENTIFYING ATTITUDES

Organizations, like individuals, differ greatly in their attitudes to stress. Some take a hard-line approach, expecting their employees to be tough enough to handle stress. Others are more caring and helpful in their responses to such problems.

43 Set up a suggestion box so employees can leave ideas for reducing stress.

44 Relieve pressure by discussing work problems openly.

45 Go for a jog or swim at lunchtime to alleviate stress.

KNOWING THE CULTURE

Take note of the predominant attitudes and behavior at work to assess your organization's approach to stress. If stress is an intrinsic part of a job, it is often easier to glamorize it than to change working practices. In certain work cultures, some stress is unavoidable: oil and mining companies expect employees to spend time away from home, and management consulting firms and investment banks expect their staff to work long hours. It is important to be able to identify unacceptable levels of workplace stress; disguising stress can make it harder to deal with the long-term effects.

CASE STUDY

The managing director of a large commercial company often boasted that he spent more time out of the office on business trips than at his desk.

When asked to develop a new product line, he worked day and night to coordinate the efforts of different departments. He flew around the world in search of information and contacts to ensure that the new line would be a success. His free time shrank, his home life suffered, he was constantly tired, and he ate poorly, but, because he knew that his company was depending on him, he continued. He began to experience severe stomach pains and was diagnosed with a peptic ulcer.

The company accepted that his condition was due to the stress of his workload. On his doctor's orders, he took a long vacation. A stress counselor was appointed by the company to help prevent future problems.

◀ **GLAMORIZING STRESS**

This case reflects a common problem. Many high-powered employees accept the heavy workload imposed by their companies and brag about their responsibilities to disguise stress and fears of failure. This company acted well by admitting that it had contributed to an unacceptably high stress level.

ASSESSING COMMITMENT TO STAFF

Some indication of a company's commitment to minimizing stress among its employees can be gleaned from its expenditure on the following:

TRAINING AND DEVELOPMENT
Companies sometimes give a figure for this in their annual accounts. If there is no figure, ask why.

REWARDS AND PROMOTION
A company that appreciates good work may give financial or other incentives, or reward by promotion.

RECRUITMENT AND SELECTION
The company that spends little time on recruitment does not mind if it loses its recruits. Candidates applying for jobs may find that a slow selection procedure or careful checking of references means that the company cares about its staff.

PENSION FUNDS
A company with a generous staff pension plan is probably serious about keeping its employees and looking after their general welfare (including their working conditions) over a long period of time.

CHANGING ATTITUDES

If your organization ignores stress in the workplace, try persuading its decision-makers to take stress seriously by making them aware of the benefits of a new attitude. For example, point out how much money stress can cost in absenteeism, and explain how much other companies have saved – several American companies claim to have reduced absenteeism by up to 60 percent by introducing counseling for staff. Remind employers that productivity usually increases when employees are happy.

46 Challenge racism or sexism within your company.

DEVISING A STRATEGY

Any organization should view devising a strategy to reduce stress as a necessary part of the cost of maintaining its most valuable asset – its workforce. The ideal strategy will depend upon the size and resources of the organization.

47 Think about introducing a pilot program before a full program.

48 Set up support systems to help stressed staff.

49 Increase investment in staff training where necessary.

THINGS TO DO

1. Identify those employees most at risk from stress.
2. Offer incentives for low absenteeism, being careful not to increase stress.
3. Promote stress awareness in in-house publications.
4. Do not allow anyone to work in-house after 7 p.m.
5. Introduce a no-smoking policy in your office.

CONSIDERING ELEMENTS

The following elements can be included in an organization's strategy for reducing stress:

- A program to increase the level of awareness throughout the organization of the enormous cost of stress within the workplace;
- A program to help employees identify the symptoms of stress both in themselves and in their colleagues;
- A counseling program to help individuals;
- A system for monitoring absenteeism (the reasons for implementing such a system, and how long it will take to implement, should be explained to all staff);
- Regular feedback reports to staff concerning the progress of the new strategy and any improvements that it brings about;
- A program of stress-preventive measures to improve the overall well-being of employees in the long term, such as the provision of sports facilities, flextime, health insurance, and regular medical checks.

50 Examine the resources of your company before deciding which strategy to use to deal with stress.

DECIDING ON LEVELS OF CHANGE

When you are devising your strategy, you need to choose a level of intervention: primary, secondary, or tertiary. Each level will bring changes to bear on a different aspect of the stress problem. Primary intervention concerns fundamental change and is rare; secondary intervention combats specific causes of stress; and tertiary intervention is concerned with individual treatment and long-term recovery.

51 Encourage healthy eating by improving in-house cafeteria lunch menus.

CONSIDERING LEVELS OF INTERVENTION

LEVEL	EXAMPLES	IMPLICATIONS
PRIMARY Involves radical change affecting an entire organization.	● Relocating from urban areas to more rural sites to improve the working environment. ● Redesigning premises, and rebuilding if necessary, to upgrade and modernize facilities.	● Companies must pay relocation expenses and set up support systems to help staff adjust. ● If staff are adversely affected while building work takes place, organizations may be obliged to offer compensation.
SECONDARY Deals with the specific causes of stress by tackling problems directly.	● Improving access to sports facilities to promote the health and fitness of employees. ● Providing an improved diet for staff where in-house cafeteria facilities exist.	● Companies may need to provide showers and changing rooms for those using sports facilities. ● In-house cafeterias should be able to offer a wide choice of meals and provide for those with special dietary requirements.
TERTIARY Provides help on an individual basis for those who suffer from stress.	● Initiating programs to help staff stop smoking or drinking; offering free medical checks. ● Providing free, confidential counseling for employees with personal problems.	● Ongoing support should be provided for staff who are trying to give up smoking or drinking. ● Free counseling services should be made available for as long as individual staff members feel that they require them.

TAKING POSITIVE ACTION

An organization that sets out to take positive action on stress at work must commit itself to the costs involved to reap the full benefits. These benefits can be measured financially as well as in terms of morale and increased productivity.

52 Be aware of your company's policy on stress management.

STARTING GRADUALLY

Taking steps to minimize stress involves change, which itself is often stressful. Remember that the costs of a stress-management program can include poor morale if the plan fails. Introduce such programs gradually to ensure that each step achieves its aim. For example, if employees are given free membership at a local gym, monitoring the staff usage will provide a good indication of how popular it is. If the facilities are well used, it might be worthwhile considering providing an on-site company gym, secure in the knowledge that it would not be a waste of money.

53 Monitor cases of absenteeism: which days of the week are the worst?

ANALYZING THE COSTS OF INTERVENTION

Intervention program

→ **Direct costs to organization**
- Expenditure on staff allocated to planning program
- Expenditure on implementation

→ **Indirect costs to organization**
- Time spent monitoring program
- Absence of workers while on course
- Poor morale if intervention fails

→ **Costs to individuals**
- Stress felt by employees upon entering program
- Buildup of workload

COMMITTING TO CHANGE

Stress management is not a quick-fix solution. To be effective, intervention must extend indefinitely, and the emphasis should gradually shift from cure of stress to prevention. Initially, the aim should be to reduce absenteeism by removing or changing the factors that create stress. Once the drop in absenteeism levels off, the program should aim to prevent it from rising again. So, in the early stages the emphasis should be on change, while later it should be on monitoring and maintaining the well-being of staff.

54 Seek out factual evidence for the effectiveness of any intervention.

MAKING CHANGES ▶

This chief executive focused on shifting the emphasis from speed to quality of work, and building team spirit. These measures increased both job satisfaction and efficiency and thereby reduced stress levels in the workforce.

CASE STUDY

Mudd & Son, a farm machinery manufacturer, appointed a forward-thinking chief executive who discovered problems with absenteeism and low morale among the workers. Employees worked on a piecework system — those who worked quickly were paid more than those who did not.

The chief executive developed a radical plan for change. The piecework system was replaced with single-status employment, in which workers were divided into grades. The better the quality of work, the higher the grade of pay. She also introduced a bonus plan rewarding workers' outstanding achievement.

Signatures of agreement were obtained from all the employees before the changes were implemented. This made the workers feel more like a team and had a positive long-term effect on output.

CASE STUDY

A large electronics company suffered a sharp drop in profit due to a high staff turnover. A team of management consultants was appointed by the directors to investigate the problem; they reported too rigid a management structure and a general lack of communication between staff and management.

Changes to the structure of the company were proposed and implemented. The consultants then suggested that all employees should go on team-building courses involving taking part in a range of outdoor activities.

Despite initial resistance from certain managers, the first course went ahead. Team members noted an increase in trust and understanding during the course. Many managers who attended the course also reported improved working relations with colleagues and junior staff.

◀ **BUILDING ON SUCCESS**

Here, company structure was found to be the cause of falling profits. Although the fundamental changes introduced to solve the problem met with resistance, the improved relations between staff and management benefited the whole company, lowering stress and ultimately raising profits.

RECLAIMING YOUR DESK

Start with your own desk to reduce stress in the workplace. Mess just makes for stress. Do not fool yourself that a messy desk is acceptable because you know where things are. Do not rely on new technology and the "paperless office" to rescue you.

55 Start each day stress-free by straightening up the night before.

POINTS TO REMEMBER

- Papers, files, and books are best stored on shelves and not your desk, leaving more work space.
- Old newspapers should be thrown away – news becomes stale fast.
- Large pieces of paper are best for writing notes. Scraps get lost.
- Records of phone calls are useless if you cannot remember when they occurred, so date notes.

56 Keep an executive toy to play with during breaks.

CLEARING OUT DEBRIS

Some people have a fear of throwing things away and of discovering that they have just disposed of the very thing they need. They therefore hoard every useless or out-of-date note. In most jobs, however, you can safely follow the three-month rule. Anything that has remained unread on your desk for three months is due for a move on to another destination – either to a file for long-term storage or into the wastepaper basket. If you have not organized your desk or done your filing for a long time, you need to be ruthless. Sort papers and notes into three distinct piles:

- Action now – work to be completed today;
- Action later – put the paper in your pending tray and complete the work within a week;
- No action – file it or throw it away.

GETTING ORGANIZED

Equip your desk with an in-box, pending tray, filing tray, and out-box – use a stacking system to save space. Make sure you sort through your pending tray and empty it once a week. Arrange your desk so that those things you use most often are most accessible. Position your computer so you do not need to twist around to use it. The monitor should be directly in front of you.

◀ **DISCARDING WASTE**
It is less stressful to have an empty desk and a full wastepaper basket than the reverse. Putting unwanted paper in the can brings a real sense of achievement. Recycle paper if possible.

IMPROVING SURROUNDINGS

Stress is affected by other visual stimuli, such as the color of our surroundings. Companies use color to create moods – in stores, reception areas, and so on. Do the same for the space around your desk. The color you select will depend on whether you prefer to be soothed or stimulated by your surroundings. Choose whichever shade is easiest for you to live and work with. Add color to your desk with flowers, plants, and family photographs.

57 Try out different room plans before you settle into a new office.

Computer monitor is angled away from harsh light

Desk is brightened up with bunch of flowers

Plant adds touch of greenery to desk

Family photo reminds you of happy times

Boxes are easily reached

Filing cabinet is close at hand

Chair swivels to face computer or writing space

▲ ENHANCING YOUR WORK SPACE

Make your workspace as aesthetically pleasing as your home. After all, you probably spend more waking hours there than you do in your home.

58 When you move to a new work space, spend time thinking how to make it more pleasant.

41

STUDYING WORK PATTERNS

Stress can be insidious and cumulative. The best way to avoid suffering from it is to learn to anticipate it. By analyzing and pinpointing events and times that regularly cause stress, it is possible to set about preventing further problems from occurring.

59 Ask a colleague to let you know when you appear to be stressed.

60 Overestimate when calculating the time that a project will take.

RECOGNIZING STRESSFUL TIMES

In the aftermath of a stressful time at work, it is easy to forget just how you managed to cope. In order to analyze stress effectively and make changes, you need to recognize your own patterns and cycles of behavior. To do this, familiarize yourself with those times of year, month, week, and day when you find you are most busy, keep records of the problems you experience, and obtain feedback from colleagues on how you perform when stressed.

ANNUAL WORK PATTERNS

Make up an annual or half-yearly chart to help you analyze annual work patterns. List all the major projects or tasks you need to complete, along with their start and end dates. Draw a line between these two dates for each task, and you will be able to see where the overlaps occur. These mark your busiest times at work and will help you plan ahead, avoiding any bottlenecks and taking vacations to coincide with quiet periods.

TASKS	JAN	FEB	MAR	APR	MAY	JUN
1	●		●			
2		●			●	
3	●			●		
4			●			●
5		●		●		

Fairly quiet time / *Very busy time* / *Quietest time*

▲ **PREPARING FOR PRESSURE**
This half-yearly chart shows the work pattern of someone whose busiest period is in March. During this time, five major tasks are ending, just beginning, or are in progress.

DAILY WORK PATTERNS

Difficulties in time management and workload prioritization are among the most common causes of stress. Once you have identified where such problems exist, you will be better able to handle them. The best way to do this is to keep a detailed daily stress diary. Prepare a "to do" list of all the tasks you have to perform each day, then use this to analyze how you are coping with your workload. Note down any problems that interfered with or prevented you from completing your tasks. This may take time to produce, but in the long term it will prevent day-to-day stress.

61 Jot down problems on a day-to-day basis, then see if a pattern emerges.

Tasks are checked off as they are completed

Increases in work being carried over to next day are monitored

Starting time of each meeting or appointment is recorded, along with its location and purpose

Tasks are prioritized in order of urgency

Essential personal tasks are listed separately

Problems are listed at the end of each day, along with ideas for resolving them

DAILY PLANNER	DATE: **6th July**	
TIME	APPOINTMENTS	PLACE
11.30	*New Project – Susan*	*Rm C*
1.00	*Lunch with Bob*	*Rm M*

To Do – WORK
1. *Read reports from last meeting* ✔
2. *Prepare agenda for Monday* ✔
3. *Review presentation graphics* ✔
4. *Review job applications*

To Do – PERSONAL
1. *Pick up clothes from dry cleaners* ✔
2. *Buy red wine for dinner* ✔

1. *Too many phone interruptions – ask Andy to handle calls or take messages.*
2. *Too much paperwork – delegate more.*
3. *Unable to review job applications - do them tomorrow.*

DAILY PLANNER	DATE
TIME	APPO
10.30	*Proje*

To Do – WORK
1. *Review job app*
2. *Schedule job in*
3. *Submit annual*
4. *Authorize batch*

To Do – PERSONAL
1. *Send birthday c*

1. *Project meeting to ensure agend*

62 Set realistic goals so that you do not feel stressed by too many failures to meet deadlines.

▲ USING A STRESS DIARY
The three main reasons for using a stress diary are to record and pinpoint stressful areas, to highlight increases in workload or other potentially stressful developments as they arise, and to have a tool for assigning priorities. Set out your stress diary as shown here, or tailor it to your preferences.

GETTING FEEDBACK

A crucial part of dealing with stress is being able to communicate effectively with the people you spend so much time with – your colleagues. One way of doing this is to ask colleagues for help and advice in response to stressful situations.

If you find yourself under stress, try to make contact with colleagues who are sympathetic and attentive listeners – those who can resist the temptation to interrupt. Even if they are not in a position to offer advice, they can still help by letting you talk through your problems and giving you support and encouragement. Ask for honest feedback about when you appear to be most stressed – do you cope with meetings calmly but appear stressed before a presentation, for example? In return, try to offer support when they are under pressure. Be an attentive listener, and encourage them to talk openly about problems.

63 Never knowingly embarrass people by asking for help they cannot give.

64 Keep negative opinions about your colleagues to yourself.

▶ GAINING CONFIDANTS
Sharing information bonds people, both in and out of the workplace. You may find that a colleague has a solution to a problem you have been having.

Share a coffee break to encourage an informal atmosphere

Put aside work while talking to colleague

ANALYZING STRESS CYCLES

Once you have analyzed your busy times of the year and recorded your daily workload for a month or so, take an overview to determine your personal daily, monthly, and yearly stress cycles. Bear in mind that the effects of cumulative pressure can increase stress. What may be easy to cope with during a quiet period will feel less possible during a crisis.

Consider which tasks you find particularly stressful – doing a large number of routine tasks may be less stressful than completing an urgent, complex one. Make yearly and daily charts of stress cycles, and use them to help you plan for a regulated stress pattern in the future.

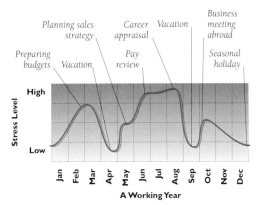

▲ A YEARLY CYCLE

The effects of long-term stress can be serious. The person to whom this chart belongs spends more than five months of the year trying to cope with high level of stress. Periods of low stress occur only when on vacation or spending time away from the office.

▼ A DAILY CYCLE

Although every day is different, a typical pattern usually emerges for most people. Consider whether you can alleviate stress, for example, by delegating more or eliminating unncessary tasks.

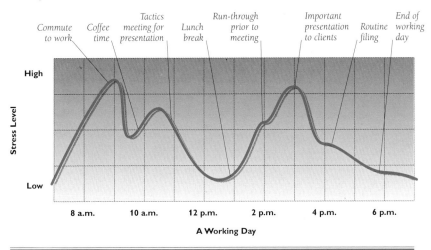

MANAGING TIME

One of the major symptoms of stress in the workplace is the feeling that there are just not enough hours in the day to do everything that needs doing. This feeling can be reduced by organizing time better with the implementation of a few simple systems.

65 Ask a member of your support staff to field calls if you have urgent work.

66 Try to take a five-minute break from your work every hour or so.

POINTS TO REMEMBER

- Objectives and goals change over time. When they do alter, the priority you give to different tasks must also change.
- A task list is not static. A sudden crisis at work or home can change it and its priorities.
- Many meetings are unnecessary.
- Indecision wastes time, but a hasty wrong decision will cause more stress in the long run.
- Checking on subordinates in minute detail takes time and will probably demoralize them.
- Telephone interruptions waste time. Tell people to call back.

PRIORITIZING OBJECTIVES

In order to manage your time better, you must begin with an assessment of your overall objectives in life. What do you want to achieve – a happy balance of work and family life? Are you actively chasing promotion in your present job? Will you settle for a position in middle management, or do you want the chief executive's office? Once you have decided, work out your long-term priorities, then plan your workload accordingly.

PLANNING TASKS

Divide your workload into three main categories: A, B, and C. Consider any tasks that are both urgent and important as A-tasks, important but slightly less urgent projects as B-tasks, and routine, low-priority jobs as C-tasks. At the end of each working day, plan out what you need to do the next day. Intersperse your important A- and B-tasks with C-tasks, such as filing or background reading, to bring variety into your day and provide relief from the constant pressures of important tasks.

67 Cross each job off your "to do" list when the job is done. It is satisfying to see a list shrink.

ALLOCATING TIME

To make the best use of your time and minimize stress, you need to manage each day carefully. Look at all the tasks you intend to do, and allocate a realistic amount of time to each. When possible, schedule one or more important (category A) tasks in the morning to avoid the pressure of having them in the back of your mind all day. Set out your schedule using a system that works well for you – whether a diary, a computer, or a time planner.

24th

8 a.m. Read mail and messages (1 hr 20 mins)	1 p.m Lun (1 h
9 a.m. Gather reports for 11 a.m. meeting with BW (40 mins)	2 p.m Mee my
10 a.m. Travel to meeting (45 mins): reread background material	3 p.m Filin (1 h
11 a.m. Meeting with BW (1 hr 15 mins)	4 p.m Plan 4.30
12 p.m. Travel back (45 mins): make notes for 2 p.m. meeting	5 p.m Ens for

Tuesday: Things to Do

- *Finish report for sales department* (**A**)
- *Prepare for meeting on Wednesday* (**A**)
- *Process invoices* (**B**)
- *Update computer lists* (**B**)
- *Check minutes of meeting for Friday* (**B**)
- *Filing* (**C**)

Urgent tasks (category A) are placed at top of list

◀ **KEEPING TASK LISTS**
Make a list of all the tasks that you have to do. Place them in order of priority, deciding where they rank according to their urgency and their importance.

▲ **RECORDING YOUR DAY**
The time you allocate to a certain task or meeting and the time you spend actually completing it are not always the same. Mark in your diary how long each task takes and the duration of each meeting (including time spent preparing and traveling). Over a period of time, note any habitual discrepancies and build extra time into future schedules to avoid pushing tasks forward, causing them to build up.

RELIEVING STRESS DURING TRAVEL TIME

Many of us spend a lot of time traveling between home and work and for meetings. Traveling can be very stressful – frequent flyers are three times more likely to suffer psychological disorders than most people – so learn a few simple exercises to help you reduce stress while on the move.

Relax wrists

◀ **STRENGTHENING WRISTS**
Grip a bar or the top of your steering wheel, and slowly roll your hands backward and forward. Repeat 10 times.

INCREASING ▶ FLEXIBILITY
Place your fingertips on a bar. Push hard so that the fingers bend back, then relax. Repeat 10 times.

Spread fingers slightly

COMMUNICATING WELL

On average, managers send and receive 178 messages every day of their working lives, while their secretaries handle even more. If this load increases without proper management, it may eventually lead to a communications gridlock.

68 Do not overload people with information that they do not need.

69 Keep a log of messages that require a reply. Follow them up.

MANAGING INFORMATION

Knowing how to communicate effectively is crucial to the success of organizations everywhere, as well as to your own peace of mind. There is a wide choice of communication tools available for modern businesses, and information can be transmitted efficiently using systems such as e-mail or fax. To minimize stress when using electronic systems, allocate sufficient time to send and reply to letters and messages, or try to delegate these tasks. Keeping on top of correspondence and processing information improves your efficiency at work and reduces stress. Good communication will also encourage a fast response from others.

CASE STUDY
Mary, a departmental manager, needed to decide between two internal candidates for a vacancy. She considered both to be capable but felt that Joe had the edge over Bill.
Instead of just appointing Joe and letting Bill hear the news from other sources, Mary arranged a meeting with Bill before announcing Joe's appointment. Mary felt that a written memo or e-mail, however tactfully composed, was the wrong way to communicate her final decision to Bill and would intensify any stress that he was feeling. She explained the reasons behind her decision, emphasizing that Bill was a valued employee, that the decision had been difficult, and that Bill would be positively considered for promotion in the future. Since Bill appreciated Mary's honesty and accepted her explanation, he did not feel bitter, undervalued, or resentful toward Joe and Mary.

◀ **COMMUNICATING EFFECTIVELY**
Methods of communication should be tailored to the audience and the situation. In this case, Mary felt that writing a memo was an inappropriate way of informing Bill of the situation. Telling him in a one-to-one meeting that he was valued, and giving him hope of a promotion in the future, helped minimize the stress of not being promoted.

KEEPING UP TO DATE

VIDEO CONFERENCING
People all over the world can participate in the
same meeting by using a video link. This saves
time and travel expenses.

E-MAIL
Electronic mail allows you to correspond using
your computer. It is the fastest and most effective
way to send messages and documents worldwide.

INTERNET
An Internet link provides immediate access
to information on every imaginable subject
(a registration fee may be required). The data can
be downloaded and saved onto your computer.

CULT
DIFFER

To communicate effectively
in business worldwide, it is
essential that you are aware of
cultural differences. In Britain
and the US, for example, you
may be able to drop in to see
someone "on spec." In Asia,
however, where communication
in business is less open and
more formal, it would be more
appropriate to arrange your
meeting properly in advance.

WORKING TOGETHER

Communicating with colleagues within a work
hierarchy can be stressful. Minimize stress by:

- Communicating and discussing issues face
  to face whenever possible to establish good
  working relationships;
- Consulting frequently with colleagues and
  other teams to get their input;
- Listening to what other people are saying,
  even if you do not agree with what is said;
- Criticizing people's ideas constructively.

TALKING OPENLY ▶
*Face-to-face meetings, such as impromptu
meetings between two colleagues, are often
more productive than written memoranda.*

70 Write faxes and letters early in
the day – your communication
skills will deteriorate as you tire.

GAINING INNER BALANCE

Although events cannot always be controlled, your reactions to them can be. Learning to respond in a balanced, appropriate fashion to events at work is a key skill in fighting stress. A bad day at the office is just that; it is not life-threatening.

71 Do not ignore your problems – acknowledge them as they arise.

MODIFYING BEHAVIOR

Behavioral patterns deeply embedded in our subconscious often surface in times of stress, even if they are not appropriate for work. For example, if a situation at work makes you feel uncomfortable and you do not take action to change it, you may find that resentment builds up and is reflected in your behavior – you may become angry and intolerant of other people. Learn to find inner balance and overcome inappropriate behavior by analyzing any feelings of unfairness and trying to discover and deal with the root of the problem.

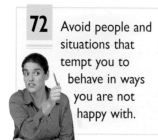

72 Avoid people and situations that tempt you to behave in ways you are not happy with.

SETTING YOUR STANDARDS

A common cause of stress is feeling guilty about doing or not doing something at work. Remember, no one is perfect, so do not ask too much of yourself. If you have very high standards and expectations, it can be difficult to accept that you have made a mistake. Try to regard mistakes as a part of a learning curve – analyze what went wrong, correct the error, and avoid repeating it. Similarly, it can be difficult to refuse work, even when the request is unreasonable. For this reason, it is important to learn to say "no" graciously. To lead a balanced life at work, you need to establish your own priorities, standards, and rights and be willing to take responsibility for your own actions.

YOUR RIGHTS

1. You have the right to make genuine mistakes without feeling guilty.

2. You have the right to refuse other people's excessive demands on your time.

HANDLING ANGER

Gaining inner balance has much to do with controlling anger. Anger is a disabling emotion that produces measurable physical sensations, such as an increase in pulse rate and a rise in blood pressure. An explosion of anger may make you feel better briefly, but it will disguise the real problem by becoming an issue in itself. If you explode unreasonably at a person or in a situation, question the root of it. Make a list of possible reasons: "I am angry because..." To control your anger successfully in the long term, explore what appears after "because."

73 Exercise can be a short-term solution to anger.

74 Be honest about your reasons for rejecting a task.

75 Try not to be pressurized into making important decisions hastily.

THINKING POSITIVELY

In order to obtain a calm, low-stress working environment, train yourself to think positively. A positive outlook and the ability to remain calm under intense pressure are likely to produce positive responses in your colleagues, which in turn will reduce the presence of stress in your team or workplace. In the same way that stress can infect a whole team, it can be eliminated by a conscious group effort to think positively.

LEARNING TO SAY NO

Some people find it difficult to say no; they are afraid of causing offense or think it might be career-threatening. Remember that accepting a task you cannot handle can be damaging. Use the phrases below to say no assertively without being aggressive.

❝ Let's arrange to meet soon and talk about this in greater detail. ❞

❝ I don't think I can give you the answer you're hoping for. ❞

❝ I am unable to take on any more commitments at the moment. ❞

MAKING TIME TO RELAX

When you are under stress, your entire body becomes tense and your posture changes. Make a conscious effort to relax your body while at work so that you can reduce tension and alleviate the damaging effects of your physical response to stress.

76 Practice yoga or a similar exercise routine to help you relax.

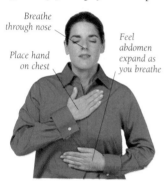

Breathe through nose

Place hand on chest

Feel abdomen expand as you breathe

▲ EXERCISE ONE
With hands on your chest and abdomen, breathe in and out through the nose, letting your abdomen expand and sink.

RELAXING AT WORK

When you spend several hours sitting at a desk or in long meetings, tension can accumulate in the upper body, particularly around the neck and shoulders, which can cause muscular aches. Follow a simple routine during the day to help you relax, release tension, and renew energy:

● Start by loosening your collar, tie, or scarf, and untying your shoelaces – or take off your shoes;
● Run through the exercises on these pages, concentrating on those you find most helpful;
● Repeat the exercises every couple of hours, rather than waiting until you feel stressed and tense. Remember, it is much easier to work toward preventing stress than to try to cure it.

Let your head fall backward

Draw fingers over collar bone

▲ EXERCISE TWO
Loosen your collar and place your hands over your shoulders. Exhale, let your head fall backward, and slowly draw your fingers over your collar bone. Repeat several times.

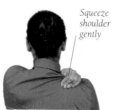

Squeeze shoulder gently

▲ EXERCISE THREE
Place your left hand on your right shoulder and squeeze gently. Hold for several seconds, then release. Repeat along the shoulder and arm. Do the same on the opposite side.

Make slow, circular movements

▲ EXERCISE FOUR
Place the fingers of both hands at the base of your skull. Apply slow, circular pressure, working gradually down your neck and then out across the shoulders.

TAKING A BREAK FROM WORKING ON SCREEN

Many people spend large amounts of time in front of computer screens. This is especially tiring for the eyes and the surrounding muscles. Take a short break from computer work every hour or so, and move or turn away from the screen. Perform the exercises shown here at regular intervals to reduce tension and prevent eye strain.

Massage gently around eyes

Move thumbs in circular motion

▲ EXERCISE ONE

Close your eyes, relax the muscles in your face, and unclench your jaw. Keeping your fingers together, place the fingertips against your forehead and gently move them in circles around your eyes. Repeat several times in one direction, then repeat in the opposite direction.

EXERCISE TWO ▲

Place your fingertips on your forehead and gently massage the temples with your thumbs.

Cup hands over eyes

EXERCISE THREE ▶

Release any tautness in your face by cupping your hands over your eyes and relaxing. Hold this position for several seconds. Do this exercise in darkness, if possible.

Gently pull head downward

Rest elbow on opposite hand

Roll shoulder backward

▲ EXERCISE FIVE

Support your left elbow on your right hand and drum the fingers of your left hand on your right shoulder blade. Repeat with your right elbow on your left hand.

▲ EXERCISE SIX

Place your hands on the top of your head. Allow your hands to pull your head gently down, then hold the position. Feel the slight stretch in the back of the neck.

▲ EXERCISE SEVEN

Lift your right shoulder and slowly rotate it backward. Repeat the exercise with your left shoulder, then rotate both shoulders together. Keep your arms loose and relaxed.

SEEING STRESS IN OTHERS

Stress can be infectious, so you need to recognize it in others before it affects the people with whom they work (including you). There are many ways of reacting to stress; learn to notice common warning signs so that you have time to decide how to react.

77 Help stressed colleagues manage their time better.

78 Ask friends of stressed colleagues to help resolve their problems.

LOOKING FOR SIGNS

The best way to recognize stress in others is to spot changes in behavior. The difference between a bad day and a sign of stress is when the abnormal behavior continues or even deteriorates. For example, the once-prompt man starts arriving late; the woman who was a good listener avoids eye contact; the soft-spoken accountant loses his temper when asked about an unpaid invoice.

NOTICING CHANGING PATTERNS OF BEHAVIOR

NORMAL

TOWARD COLLEAGUES
- Greets colleagues on arrival.
- Has lunch with colleagues.
- Has a friendly manner.
- Asks for opinions.

TOWARD THE ORGANIZATION
- Keeps work space clean and neat.
- Files paperwork in an orderly fashion.
- Knows where to find things.
- Deals with correspondence immediately.

TOWARD OWN APPEARANCE
- Is smartly dressed.
- Wears clean and well-pressed clothes.
- Looks well-groomed.
- Maintains good personal hygiene.

STRESSED

TOWARD COLLEAGUES
- Sits at work in silence.
- Ignores opinions.
- Becomes irritable.
- Lunches alone.

TOWARD THE ORGANIZATION
- Works in a chaotic fashion.
- Scatters papers everywhere.
- Takes 15 minutes to find anything.
- Leaves in-box full of correspondence.

TOWARD OWN APPEARANCE
- Wears clothes unsuited to the job.
- Wears dirty and wrinkled clothing.
- Looks unkempt.
- Does not appear to care about appearance.

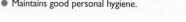

EXPLORING REASONS

Once you have noticed some signs of stress in a colleague, you need to start thinking about the reasons for it. Consider as many options as possible – from problems at home to any difficult relationships in the workplace. Remember that the factors that put you under greatest stress may not affect others to the same extent. Once you have pinpointed likely causes, assess whether or how you can help your colleague. Often, only that person can help himself, and all you can do is ensure he is not put under additional pressure.

ANALYZING TEAM STRESS

Staff who work in teams, brought together to do a particular task, can suffer from specific pressures related to working in a group. For example, if an informal hierarchy develops, some may not approve of the self-appointed leader, or team members may find it stressful to work with people who have different work patterns to their own. Take time to meet teams and individuals so that you are aware of team dynamics and can anticipate problems. You may need to alter working methods and the division of tasks within a team if stress persists.

79 Give colleagues under stress some relaxation tips.

80 Offer help only if you have time to follow it up.

AVERTING PRESSURES

You can try to minimize stresses and pressures among those you work with by using open, flexible working practices. The better communication flows, the more likely it is that stress is recognized and defused. Try the following methods of involving people and reducing levels of anxiety:

● Keep staff and colleagues informed about all decisions that may affect them;

● Encourage participation in planning;

● Set aside time each week to ask for comments and suggestions and to give feedback.

ANALYZING PERSONALITY

The effects of stress are closely linked to individual personality. The same level of stress affects different people in different ways, and each person has different ways of coping. Recognizing these personality types means that more focused help can be given.

81 Suggest that your colleagues try to view problems as opportunities.

UNDERSTANDING TYPES

82 Respect other opinions – do not feel you always need to be right.

Research in the 1960s into the effects of stress on the heart found that some patients with similarities in personality were more prone to heart disease. These people were described as Type A, while those less at risk were classed as Type B. The former are competitive and hard-driving and are likely to seek out positions of responsibility. Whether their health is at risk because they are in high-stress jobs or whether high-risk jobs encourage Type-A behavior is unclear, but these people may need more support.

IDENTIFYING PERSONALITY TYPES A AND B

Listed here are some of the classic traits and behavior patterns associated with personality Types A and B. It is rare to find someone who is a perfect Type A or B – many people exhibit characteristics of both – but those with mostly Type-A traits often cope badly under pressure. If you detect Type-A tendencies in colleagues, they may be at risk from stress and should consider strategies to deal with this.

- Type-A personalities may show the following tendencies: competitiveness; hastiness; aggressiveness; impatience; assertiveness; perfectionism; restlessness; punctuality; seeking attention.
- Type-B personalities may show the following tendencies: noncompetitiveness; placidity; patience; being laid-back; being relaxed; contentment; enjoying routine; tardiness; being happy to work unnoticed.

RECOGNIZING STRATEGIES

Strategies for coping with stress can be divided into two main categories: adaptive and maladaptive. If colleagues exhibit adaptive behavior, they are probably dealing positively with a problem, talking about it, and actively seeking help. If they are behaving maladaptively, they may be causing themselves greater stress by ignoring their problem and trying to carry on as normal. This type of behavior, known as being "in denial," is often associated with competitive, Type-A personalities.

83 Identify and enlist the help of stress-free, supportive members of staff.

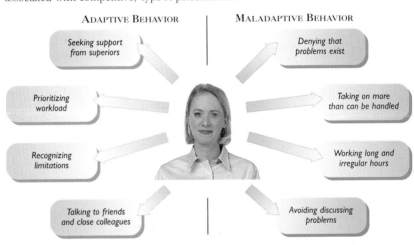

ADAPTIVE BEHAVIOR

Seeking support from superiors

Prioritizing workload

Recognizing limitations

Talking to friends and close colleagues

MALADAPTIVE BEHAVIOR

Denying that problems exist

Taking on more than can be handled

Working long and irregular hours

Avoiding discussing problems

NOTICING CHANGES

When colleagues are adversely affected by stress, their behavior may change dramatically, and negative characteristics may be intensified. For example, a person who normally tends to be impatient – and may be known for "not suffering fools gladly" – may find that this degenerates to a point where they cannot control their temper, leading to explosive and destructive temper tantrums. Watch for such warning signals in your colleagues.

▲ **ASSESSING BEHAVIOR**
Adaptive and maladaptive behaviors are two ways of dealing with stress. The former tends to lead to problems being resolved, while the latter can increase problems.

84 Advise colleagues to concentrate on one task at a time.

HELPING OTHERS

Once you have recognized that someone is under stress and have started to understand the reasons for it, the hardest part begins: making that person aware of what you have observed and encouraging them to take corrective action.

85 Keep a note of situations that trigger stress in your colleagues.

UNDERSTANDING TENSION AREAS

Always be aware of the work your staff needs to cope with on a daily, weekly, monthly, and annual basis. You will then better understand the pressures they may be under at any given time. Tensions may arise as a result of competition between colleagues whose jobs are either very similar or have several overlapping aspects. In most instances, you need not worry about competitive tensions; encourage those directly involved to work things out between themselves. If you become aware that a situation may escalate into a problem, prevent role conflict by defining clearly what is expected of each party.

86 Ensure that staff working together are compatible.

PREVENTING A CONFLICT OF ROLES

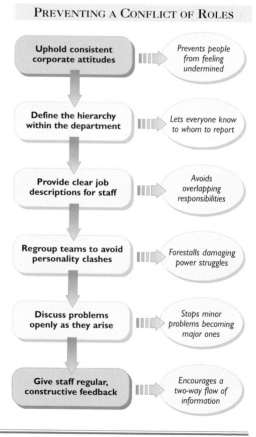

Uphold consistent corporate attitudes → *Prevents people from feeling undermined*

Define the hierarchy within the department → *Lets everyone know to whom to report*

Provide clear job descriptions for staff → *Avoids overlapping responsibilities*

Regroup teams to avoid personality clashes → *Forestalls damaging power struggles*

Discuss problems openly as they arise → *Stops minor problems becoming major ones*

Give staff regular, constructive feedback → *Encourages a two-way flow of information*

ASSESSING RELATIONSHIPS

In many ways, the personal relationships that exist between colleagues are just as important as their professional relationships. As a manager, try to be aware of who gets along with whom. Once you have a clear understanding of the personal relationships around you, you can start to build up teams of people who work well together.

87 List all the people who may be able to help a colleague under stress.

HELPING OTHERS ADMIT TO STRESS

Sometimes a subtle, indirect approach is needed to help others admit to stress. Social relationships can cut across the roles and hierarchies found in the workplace – in some cases it may be appropriate to involve a third party. This is one point where you will find it useful to know who gets on well with whom. A discreet word with the right person can reap great rewards and is a helpful and tactful way – as a first attempt, at least – to bring someone's attention to their own stress levels. This will avoid the person's stress becoming an official issue and may enable them to remedy the situation. A more direct approach may be necessary if this does not work.

88 Encourage staff to be supportive of one another.

BARRIERS TO ADMITTING STRESS

FOR MANAGERS

● Managers may believe that their authority rests to some extent on appearing infallible.
● Managers may not want to admit that they are under stress for fear that it will undermine their leadership.

FOR COLLEAGUES

● Colleagues may not want to expose weaknesses to each other in case they are exploited in the future.
● Friendships may suffer between colleagues who become rivals for the same promotion.

FOR SUBORDINATES

● Subordinates may feel that their careers will suffer if they show signs of stress to staff who have a degree of control over their jobs.
● Subordinates may not want to show signs of weakness to senior staff.

IMPLEMENTING ACTION

Once stress is recognized and acknowledged, devise a strategy to help the sufferer deal with it. Ask both subordinates and colleagues if they have any suggestions on how to reduce their own workload, for example, by delegating some aspects of their role to someone else. Discuss all possible courses of action that can be taken. Always endorse alternative arrangements so that the person under stress does not feel they are letting others down.

89 Suggest that your meetings should last no longer than half an hour.

FINDING A SOLUTION TO A PROBLEM

Problem

- List difficulties
- Consider causes
- Discuss remedies
- Agree on action

Solution

SHARING KNOWLEDGE AND EXPERIENCE

It is sometimes possible to indicate subtly certain courses of action that can be taken to reduce stress levels without suggesting that any one individual member of staff has a problem. For example, everyone knows that time management can cause problems, so it is a good idea to pool your knowledge and ideas on how to streamline the day. Be blatant about introducing time-saving techniques and encourage awareness of stress patterns. Make general statements such as "I couldn't survive without my wallchart," or "I always need at least 15 minutes before I go into a meeting to prepare myself." Make colleagues aware that all brilliant leaders need their crutches. Mention areas that you personally find stressful and share solutions that have been successful for you.

SUPPORTING OTHERS

Occasionally you will need to support others who are in the middle of a stressful situation. Take a calm, logical approach and follow these steps:

● Discuss the problems that the individual is experiencing, then determine the underlying causes of their stress – find out whether their problem is work-related or personal;

● Having analyzed the type of stress from which the person is suffering, discuss what help they would find most useful – this might take the form of work-related help (such as training), emotional help (such as counseling), or medical help (such as treatment for a condition brought on or aggravated by stress);

● Assist the individual in finding the help they need. Be prepared to suggest alternative solutions in case they are unhappy with your initial suggestions and recommendations.

90 Ask colleagues to prioritize tasks in their diaries.

91 When talking with a colleague, banish all interruptions.

▼ **TAKING TIME TO LISTEN**
Any discussion with a stressed colleague or subordinate should take place in confidence in a meeting room. Make as much time available as is necessary.

Sit at right angles to the person under stress to make them feel at ease

Keep body language open to encourage free discussion

Arms forming barrier across chest suggest diffidence

TAKING ACTION AT HOME

Stress felt at work is guaranteed to affect home life, which will have a detrimental impact on family and friends. Learn to take time off, relax, develop interests, and eat well.

TAKING TIME OFF

Taking stress home from the office has a destructive effect on home life, and vice versa. The two can combine to form a vicious circle with no escape. Remember: to make any stress-reducing action effective, it must be complemented by taking some time off.

92 Plan activities for each weekend. Try not to let the days just drift past.

MAKING TIME FOR OTHERS

The first step toward reducing stress at home is to allow plenty of time for family matters. Make your family aware that vacations with them are sacred, and show friends that they are worth more than just a quick drink on a Friday night every other month. Make sure that people at work are aware of your commitments to your family – your child's sports day, for example, or a special anniversary – and that they have priority over work issues. Simple things count for a lot: make an effort to have lunch regularly with your partner or time to throw a ball around with your children.

▲ SPENDING TIME ALONE
If you do not enjoy your own company, you are condemned to be dependent on others. Learn to enjoy yourself by yourself.

PLANNING AN ANTISTRESS DAY

The world is changing faster than ever, and the speed of these changes is putting us all under unprecedented pressure. It is important that we regularly visit the stability zones – dependable activities such as walking the dog, going for a bicycle ride, reading a book, watering plants, washing the car, or watching a television show full of familiar, predictable characters – that make us feel comfortable with ourselves and convince us that all is well with the world. There is nothing better for recharging flat batteries than a well-planned antistress day. Organize your activities well in advance, take a day off from work, and plan out your time. If you have any children, arrange for them to stay with some relatives or friends, or include them in your plans for your relaxation day.

▲ GETTING EXERCISE

Exercise is a major stress reliever. Take up a noncompetitive sport, and build your strength gradually.

MORNING

Make sure that when you wake, you wake naturally. Do not leap out of bed, but savor the prospect of the day ahead. Once you do get up, take a few minutes to do some simple stretching exercises. Drink a glass of water before enjoying a light breakfast, which should include at least one special treat.

AFTERNOON

For some, a noncompetitive day on the golf course might be the most pleasurable thing to follow breakfast. Others may want to set out for some retail therapy – a spot of shopping and a leisurely lunch with a good friend. Try to leave the car at home and walk, ride a bicycle, or use public transportation.

EARLY EVENING

Resist the temptation to read the papers or watch the news on television. In the treatment of stress, no news is good news. A key feature of any antistress day is not knowing what is going on in the rest of the world – it will carry on without you. Read a book, curl up with a video, listen to music, or go to the movies.

NIGHT

Have a leisurely bath, and pamper yourself with body oils. Listen to music while dressing slowly for a relaxed dinner in a restaurant with your partner or a friend. Take a taxi, and do not worry about time. When you get home, have a cup of soothing herbal tea before going to bed and drifting off to sleep.

LEARNING TO RELAX

Relaxing completely is not simply doing nothing: it is a technique that can soon be learned. Take some time out for a few lessons, and you will then find it easy – and pleasurable – to enjoy a regular period of relaxation in your busy daily routine.

93 Listen to your favorite comedian. Laughter will help you relax.

BEGINNING TO RELAX

It is not always easy to relax at home, since there are so many demands on our time – telephones ringing, meals to be cooked, clothes to be ironed, and so on. Find a tranquil place in the house, and set aside a period of uninterrupted time to do the simple relaxation exercise shown below. You may choose to try it out first thing in the morning, perhaps before breakfast, or last thing at night, just before you go to bed. Wear some loose, baggy clothes that do not restrict your movement. Place a rug or mat on the floor, along with a cushion, then lie down and begin the exercise.

94 Avoid eating or drinking heavily just before you go to bed.

▼ 1. TENSING YOUR BACK MUSCLES

Lying flat on the floor, stretch your arms out by either side. Use the muscles in your shoulders, back, and buttocks to raise your torso slowly off the ground. Feel the tension in your body, then hold the position for the count of five.

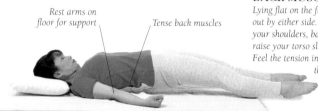

Rest arms on floor for support   Tense back muscles

2. RELAXING ▶ YOUR BODY

Slowly lower your back to the floor and relax, breathing slowly and deeply. Repeat as required.

Breathe through nose   Relax feet

LEARNING TO MEDITATE

Meditation has been used for centuries to counteract the effects of stress. Sit on the floor in an upright position with your legs crossed, arms resting on your thighs and palms facing upward. Close your eyes and breathe through your nostrils, focusing on the air coming in and out of your body. Sit for a few minutes, quietly aware of your body. After a while, you will feel the tension start to ease away.

Repeat a word or phrase over and over in your mind

Breathe gently from diaphragm

CALMING DOWN ▶
The goal of meditation is the attainment of a state of calm awareness. If you find it difficult to concentrate at first, persevere, and slowly your mind will clear.

SEEKING HELP

People who have trouble in relaxing may find relaxation therapies helpful. The many systems available include:
ALEXANDER TECHNIQUE: learning how to use the body in everyday tasks to minimize pain, stress, and injury.
AROMATHERAPY: massaging the body with essential oils.
FLOTATION: floating in a water tank filled with a solution of mineral salts.
SHIATSU: using finger pressure on certain areas of the body to relieve stress and tension.

SLEEPING BETTER

Everybody needs a different amount of sleep. For adults, the average is seven to eight hours a night, but many high-achieving people claim to survive on four or five. Stress can cause us to sleep less than we need over a prolonged period and to sleep poorly. To improve the quality of your sleep, make sure you relax before you go to bed. Switch off from all stimulating activities – especially work – at least two hours beforehand. Try meditating. Read some light fiction. Listen to some music, or watch television. Have a warm, milky drink last thing at night, or try an infusion of one of the many herbal plants that are thought to aid sleep, such as chamomile, valerian, or passiflora.

95 When lying down to relax your body, start by relaxing your toes, and work your way upward.

DEVELOPING INTERESTS

Finding a balanced lifestyle is essential to our overall well-being. Physical activities such as aerobics or tennis can concentrate the mind and help reduce the outward symptoms of stress, while hobbies such as painting can provide emotional calm.

96 Join an evening class every year, and start to learn something new.

97 Ask your company to take corporate membership in a nearby sports club.

TAKING UP NEW HOBBIES

Choose an activity that you really enjoy doing to beat stress. The right pastime can be so absorbing that it helps you switch off from everything else and so engrossing that it becomes as refreshing as sleep. A hobby also helps boost self-esteem. After a day at the office when nothing seemed to go right, you can head for your hobby and lose yourself in your skill. Some people's hobbies have even become their livelihoods. Accountants have become avid beekeepers; lawyers have turned to furniture restoration. Hobbies can be portable – many people are able to combine their hobbies with vacations, such as a cycling trip in the Andes, for example, golfing in Portugal, or perhaps a guided tour of the flora and fauna of Australia.

◀ **RELAXING WITH A NEW HOBBY**
Remember that a hobby is meant to be a pleasure, not a chore – go out and paint only when you feel like it. If you cannot find the time to finish that art course, do not worry. Do the best you can, and squeeze enjoyment out of it.

GETTING MORE EXERCISE

Exercise is widely recognized as beneficial in reducing anxiety and improving sleep. However, take care, since those who exercise vigorously while highly stressed are prone to injury. Remember to start gradually and build up to a regular exercise regime. When planning your sporting activities, build in the time that it takes to travel, change, and shower. Some sports, such as tennis and golf, combine physical exercise with social activity – which is in itself a stress minimizer. Brisk walking, swimming, and aerobics classes are all effective in improving the cardiovascular system. The chart below shows the effects of different sports on stamina, flexibility, and strength. Use it to choose one or more sports activities that would suit you.

98 Take a vacation that allows you to pursue a hobby.

99 When taking up a new form of exercise, start with lessons from a qualified instructor.

Key
★ ★ ★ ★ *Excellent effect*   ★ ★ *Beneficial effect*
★ ★ ★ *Very good effect*   ★ *Minimal effect*

CHOOSING THE RIGHT SPORT

ACTIVITY	STAMINA	FLEXIBILITY	STRENGTH
BASKETBALL	★ ★ ★	★ ★ ★ ★	★ ★ ★
BOWLING	★	★ ★	★ ★
CYCLING	★ ★ ★ ★	★ ★	★ ★ ★
GOLF	★ ★	★ ★	★
RUNNING	★ ★ ★ ★	★ ★	★ ★
SOCCER	★ ★ ★	★ ★ ★	★ ★
SQUASH	★ ★ ★ ★	★ ★ ★ ★	★ ★ ★
SWIMMING	★ ★ ★	★ ★ ★	★ ★ ★
TENNIS	★ ★ ★	★ ★ ★	★ ★
WALKING	★ ★	★	★ ★

IMPROVING DIET

W*e are what we eat. When we are under stress, we tend to fill ourselves with convenience food, which can be synonymous with "junk." Eating well must be part of any serious program to reduce stress levels. Make a start by minimizing bad habits.*

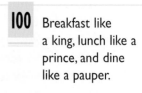

100 Breakfast like a king, lunch like a prince, and dine like a pauper.

REDUCING BAD HABITS

Monitoring what you consume and when may reveal bad habits that have crept into your diet. The one glass of wine with dinner easily becomes most of a bottle, while the pizza once a week becomes a daily meal. Try to adopt a well thought-out and balanced diet, replacing convenience foods with healthier alternatives.

Certain foods have been linked with poor overall health. Avoid foods high in saturated fats, such as meat, cheese, butter, and eggs. Use olive oil or sunflower oil for cooking, and steam, bake, or broil food rather than fry it. Eat plenty of oily fish, such as salmon, and try a soy-based meal in place of meat. Reduce your daily intake of caffeine by replacing coffee and tea with water or juice. Drink at least eight glasses of water every day.

▲ **BALANCING YOUR DIET**
Instead of reheating convenience foods when you come home from work, why not prepare yourself a nutritious plate of pasta? It is just as easy and quick to cook as fast foods and is a much healthier alternative.

DO'S AND DON'TS

✔ Do eat small meals at regular intervals rather than one enormous dinner.

✔ Do determine your optimum weight, and then aim to stick to it.

✔ Do aim for moderation in all things.

✘ Don't snack between meals, especially on sugary foods, which drain the body of valuable nutrients.

✘ Don't keep sweets in the house.

✘ Don't eat a lot of salt, sugar, or white bread.

101 Eat a crisp, raw carrot if you feel the urge to eat between meals.

Essential Components of a Healthy Diet

Components

Good Sources

Vitamins and Minerals
Vitamins help the body function properly. There is an official recommended daily intake for every vitamin. Minerals, as important to good health as vitamins, consist of some 20 chemical elements.

Vitamins come from many sources: Vitamin C from citrus fruits, tomatoes, melons, strawberries; Vitamin D from green vegetables, oily fish, milk, eggs; Vitamin B1 from meat, yeast, legumes. Leafy vegetables and fish are good sources of minerals.

Carbohydrates
This large group of foodstuffs includes sugars and starches. Nutritionists generally recommend that carbohydrates should make up approximately 55 percent of a typical healthy diet.

Carbohydrates are found in whole-grain bread, candy, cookies, pasta, apples, corn, cereal, baked and red kidney beans, lentils, green peppers, dried apricots, bananas, baked or boiled potatoes, unsalted nuts, dried fruit, brown rice.

Proteins from Plants
The body needs proteins in the form of amino acids for cell growth and repair and to make enzymes for antibodies and hormones. All fruits and vegetables contain a certain amount of these proteins.

Good sources of plant proteins are peas, beans, grains, lentils, seeds, and potatoes. Some plant proteins do not contain all or enough essential amino acids, so vegetarians should try to eat a mixture of nuts or grains and peas or beans.

Proteins from Animals
Proteins of animal origin provide complete protein. In other words, they contain the whole range of essential amino acids that the human body needs and in the appropriate proportions.

Red meats are a source of animal proteins that are essential for a healthy functioning body. These proteins are also found in other sources, including poultry, fish, eggs, and dairy products such as cheese, butter, milk, and yogurt.

Fats
Fats are a key source of energy – we need fat to function efficiently. A healthy diet should consist of 30 percent fat, but too much can cause serious health problems such as heart disease and obesity.

Fish, chicken, vegetable oils, and avocados are good sources of light polyunsaturated and monosaturated fats. Butter, meats, eggs, cream, and whole milk are high in saturated fat, which is harder for the body to process and less healthy than polyunsaturated or monosaturated fat.

INDEX

A

absenteeism:
  alcohol abuse, 8
  back pain, 31
  causes of, 7, 10
  counseling services for, 35
  measuring stress in
  organizations, 15
  monitoring, 38
  statistics, 14
  stress-management
  programs, 36, 37
adaptive behavior, 57
adrenaline, 7, 14
aging populations, 21
air conditioning, 31
alcohol, 8, 13
Alexander Technique, 65
analyzing jobs, 26–27
anger, controlling, 51
antistress days, 63
appearance, difference in, 54
aromatherapy, 65
assertiveness, saying no, 51
attitudes to stress, 34–35

B

back muscles, relaxing, 64
balance, inner, 50–51
behavior:
  coping strategies, 57
  patterns of, 50
  seeing stress in others, 54
  symptoms of stress, 13
blue-collar workers, 27
boredom, 27
breathing, relaxation, 52, 65

C

carbohydrates, 69
careers, diversifying, 25
cars, commuting by, 33
causes of stress, 20–33
change:
  changing practices, 24–25
  in organizations, 22–23
  in society, 20–21
children, 9, 33, 62
clerical workers, 27

colleagues:
  communicating with, 48–49
  feedback from, 44
  helping, 58–61
  seeing signs of stress in, 54–55
  working relationships with, 29
color, in working
  environment, 41
communication, 48–49
  feedback, 38, 44, 58
commuting, 33
competition, between
  colleagues, 58
computers:
  e-mail, 49
  eye strain, 53
  home offices, 25
  learning to use, 24
  support networks for, 31
  in working environment, 40, 41
coping strategies, 57
cortisol, 7
cost-cutting, 22
counseling:
  absenteeism, 35
  stress-management
  programs, 38, 61
cultural differences:
  communication, 49
  respect for age, 28

D

daily life, 32–33
decision-making, 9
delegation, 27, 50
demographic changes, 20–21
denial, maladaptive behaviour, 57
depression, 8
desks, organizing, 40–41
diaries:
  planning day, 47
  stress diaries, 43
diet, 68–69
divorce, 9
drug abuse, 8

E

eating habits, 8, 68
electronic communication
  systems, 49

e-mail, 49
emotions:
  controlling anger, 51
  symptoms of stress, 8, 13
environment, workplace, 31, 41
exercises:
  hands, 47
  for relaxation, 52–53, 63, 67
eye strain, 53

F

family life, 9, 62
faxes, 49
feedback:
  helping colleagues, 58
  helping yourself, 44
  stress-management
  programs, 38
financial jobs, 26
flattening, 22, 28
flexible working hours, 33
flotation therapy, 65
food, 68–69
friendships, 32

G

gender roles, 21
globalization, 22
guilt, feeling, 50
gyms, providing, 36

H

health, effects of stress on, 8
heart disease, 8, 14, 56
helping others, 58–61
hierarchy:
  role conflict in, 58
  in teams, 55
  working relationships, 29
hobbies, 66
home life, 9, 62–69
home offices, 25
hormones, 7
human body, effects of stress, 7

I

information, communication,
  48–49
information technology, 22, 24
inner balance, 50–51